Piano Accompaniments to
Everybody's Favorite Songs
for High Voice
Vol. 1

To access audio visit:
www.halleonard.com/mylibrary

Enter Code
7415-2446-3283-9616

ISBN 978-1-59615-497-1

EXCLUSIVELY DISTRIBUTED BY

HAL•LEONARD®

7777 W. BLUEMOUND RD. P.O. BOX 13819 MILWAUKEE, WI 53213

Visit Hal Leonard Online at
www.halleonard.com

JOHN WUSTMAN

John Wustman is one of the few accompanists in this country who has achieved renown and critical acclaim in this most challenging of art forms. Mr. Wustman has developed that rare quality of bringing a strength and character to his accompaniments which create a true collaboration between the singer and the pianist. And this is as it should be, for in the art song especially, the piano part is not a mere rhythmic and tonal background, but an integral part of the composer's intent and creation. Thus, on these recordings, Mr. Wustman provides not only the necessary accompaniment, but also through his artistry, a stylistic and interpretive suggestion for the study of the music.

Among the many artists he has accompanied in past years are Gianna d'Angelo, Irina Arkhipova, Montserrat Caballe, Regine Crespin, Nicolai Gedda, Evelyn Lear, Mildred Miller, Anna Moffo, Brigit Nilsson, Jan Peerce, Roberta Peters, Elizabeth Schwarzkopf, Renata Scotto, Cesare Siepi, Giulietta Simionato, Thomas Stewart, Cesare Valetti, and William Warfield.

Mr. Wustman has become known to millions of television viewers as the accompanist to Luciano Pavarotti in his many appearances in concert and recital.

Everybody's Favorite Songs

FOR

High Voice
Vol. 1

My Heart Ever Faithful

Mein Gläubiges, Herze, Frohlocke

J.S. Bach

Andante con moto

Mein gläu - biges Her - ze, froh-lo - cke, sing', scher-ze,
My heart ev-er faith-ful, Sing prais - es, be joy - ful,

mein gläu - bi - ges Her - ze, froh-
My heart ev - er faith - ful, Sing

lo - cke, sing', scher-ze, froh-lo - cke, sing', scher - ze, dein Je - sus ist nah; mein
prais - es, be joy - ful, sing prais - es, be joy ful, Thy Je - sus is near; My

gläu - bi - ges Her-ze, froh-lo - cke, sing', scher-ze, fro - lo - cke, sing', scher-ze, dein
heart ev - er faith-ful, Sing prais - es, be joy - ful, sing prais - es, be joy - ful, Thy

Je - sus ist nah!
Je - sus is near!

Weg Jam - mer, weg Kla - gen, weg Jam - mer, weg Kla - gen, ich
A - way with com - plain - ing, a - way with com - plain - ing, Faith

will euch nur sa - gen, mein Je - sus ist da; weg Jam - mer, weg Kla - gen, ich
ev - er main - tain - ing, My Je - sus is here; A - way with com - plain - ing, Faith

will euch nur sa - gen, mein Je - sus ist da, mein Je - sus ist da;
ev - er main - tain - ing, My Je - sus is here, my Je - sus is here;

weg
A-

5

Jam - mer, weg Kla - gen, weg Jam - mer, weg Kla - gen, ich will_ euch nur sa - gen, mein
way_ with com-plain - ing, a - way_ with com-plain - ing, Faith ev - er main-tain - ing, My

Je - sus ist da! Mein gläu - bi-ges Her - ze, froh - lo - cke, sing', scher - ze,
Je - sus is here! My heart_ ev-er faith-ful, Sing prais - es, be joy - ful,

mein gläu - bi-ges Her - ze, froh-
My heart_ ev-er faith - ful, Sing

lo - cke, sing', scher - ze, froh - lo - cke, sing', scher - ze, dein Je - sus ist da, froh-
prais - es, be joy - ful, sing prais - es, be joy - ful, Thy Je - sus is here, Sing

6

lo-cke, sing', scherze, froh - lo - - - cke, sing', scher -
praises, be joy-ful, sing prais - - - es, be joy -

- ze, mein gläu - bi-ges Her - ze, froh - lo - cke, sing', scher - ze, froh -
- ful, My heart _ ev - er faith-ful, Sing prais - es, be joy - ful, sing

lo - cke, sing', scher - ze, dein Je - sus ist da!
prais - es, be joy - ful, Thy Je - sus is here!

7

Ave Maria
Sacred Melody adapted to the First Prelude of J.S. Bach

Charles Gounod

Andante con moto

A - - - - ve Ma - ri - - - - a, - - - - - -
A - - - - ve Ma - ri - - - - a! - - - - - -

gra - - - ti - a ple - - na,
Thou_____ high-ly fa - - vored,

8

9

Ave Maria

English adapted from the first chapter of St. Luke

Franz Schubert,
Op, 52, No., 6

Molto lento *(sehr langsam)*

A - - ve Ma - ri - - a! Maid - en
A - - ve Ma - ri - - a! Jung - frau
A - - ve Ma - ri - - a! gra - ti-a ple -

mild, Ah! lis - ten to a maid-en's prayer:___ For Thou canst hear a-mid the
mild, er - hö - re ei-ner Jung-frau Fle - hen, aus die - sem Fel-sen starr und
na, Ma - ri - a, gra - ti-a ple - na, Ma - ri - a, gra-ti-a ple -

a!
a!
a!

A — ve Ma-ri — — a! Un — de —
A — ve Ma-ri — — a! Un — be —
A — ve Ma-ri — — a! Ma — ter De —

fil'd! The flint - y couch where-on we're sleep - ing Shall seem with down of ei - der
fleckt! Wenn wir auf die - sen Fels hin - sin - ken zum Schlaf und uns dein Schutz be -
i, O - ra pro no - bis pec-ca - to - ri-bus, O - ra, o-ra pro no -

pil'd, If Thou a-bove sweet watch art keep - - ing. The
deckt, wird weich der har - te Fels uns dün - - ken. Du
bis, O - ra, o-ra— pro no - bis pec-ca-to - ri-bus, nunc

14

murk - y cav - ern's air so heav - y   Shall
lü - - chelst, Ro - sen-duf - te we - hen.   *in*
et   in   ho - ra_____ mor - tis,   *in*

breathe of balm, if Thou hast smil'd;   O
die - ser dumpfen Fel - sen - kluft;   *o*
ho - ra mor - tis no - stræ,   in

Maid - en, hear a maid-en plead-ing,   O
Mut - ter, hör' des Kin-des Fle - hen,   *o*
ho - ra mor - tis, mor-tis no - stræ,   in

Moth - er, hear a sup-pliant child!   A -
Jung-frau, ei - ne Jungfrau ruft!   *A -*
ho - ra mor - tis no - stræ,   A

ve Ma - ri - -
ve Ma - ri - -
ve Ma - ri - -

a!
a!
a!

thy   dear guid - ance rec - on - cil'd;   Then
uns   dein heil'- ger Trost an-weht;   du
be - ne - di -   - ctus,   et

hear, oh Maid, a sim-ple maid-en,   And for a fa - ther hear a child!
Jung-frau wol - le hold dich nei-gen   dem Kind, das für den Va - ter fleht!
be - ne - di - ctus fru-ctus ven-tris,   ventris tu - i, Je -   sus.

fp   *pp*

A -   ve Ma - ri -   a!
A -   ve Ma - ri -   a!
A -   ve Ma - ri -   a!

dim.

Wiegenlied
Cradle Song

Karl Simrock

Johannes Brahms
Op. 49, No. 4

Original key Eb major

Dolce con moto

Gu-ten A - bend, gut' Nacht, mit Ro-sen be-dacht, mit Näg-lein be-steckt, schlüpf' un-ter die Deck': Mor-gen früh, wenn Gott will, wirst du wie-der ge-weckt, mor-gen früh, wenn Gott will, wirst du wie-der ge-weckt!

Lullaby and good night! With roses bedight,
Creep into thy bed, There pillow thy head.
If God will, thou shalt wake when the morning doth break,
If God will, thou shalt wake when the morning doth break.

Lullaby and good night; Those blue eyes close tight;
Bright angels are near, So sleep without fear.
They will guard thee from harm With fair Dreamland's sweet charm,
They will guard thee from harm With fair Dreamland's sweet charm.

Gu-ten A - bend, gut' Nacht, von Eng-lein be-wacht, die zei-gen im Traum dir Christ-kind-leins Baum: Schlaf' nun se - lig und süss, schau' im Traum's Pa - ra - dies! schlaf' nun se - lig und süss, schau' im Traum's Pa - ra - dies!

19

Dedication
Widmung
(Wolfgang Müller.)

Andante con moto

Op. 14, No. 1

Original key

O dan - ke nicht für die - se Lie - der, mir ziemt es,
Nay, thank me not that songs I sing thee, Thanks there shall

dank - bar Dir zu sein; Du gabst sie mir,— ich ge - be
be, but they'll be mine! 'Twas thou that gav'st,— I do but

wie - der was jetzt und einst und e - wig Dein.
bring thee What was and ev - er shall be thine.

Dein sind sie alle ja gewesen, aus Deiner
I've look'd in thy dear eyes, and tak-en The truth that

lieben Augen Licht hab' ich sie treu-lich ab-ge-
there a-lone be-longs; Then tell me not, I was mis-

le-sen, kennst Du die eig-nen Lie-der
tak-en, Dost thou not know thine own sweet

nicht? kennst Du die eig-nen Lie-der nicht?
songs? Dost thou not know thine own sweet songs?

(Henry G. Chapman.)

21

Songs My Mother Taught Me

Als die alte Mutter

Soprano or Tenor

Anton Dvořák
Op. 55, No. 4

Jetzt, wo__ ich die Klei -
Now I__ teach my__ chil -

nen sel - ber üb' im__ San - - ge, rie - selt's
dren ach me - lo - dious__ meas - - ure; Oft the

in den__ Bart_____ oft, rie - selt's oft_____ von der
(mir__ vom__ Au - - ge, rie - selts oft mir auf die
tears__ are__ flow - - ing, oft they flow_____ from my

brau - nen__ Wan - - ge.
brau - ne__ Wan - - ge.)
mem - ry's treas - ure.

23

None but the lonely heart

Nur wer die Sehnsucht kennt

Peter Ilyitch Tschaikovsky
Op. 6, No. 6

25

part-ed far From joy and glad - ness, A - lone_____ and part-ed
ab - ge-trennt von al - ler Freu - de, al - lein_____ und ab - ge-

far_____ From joy and glad - ness. My sens - es
trennt_____ von al - ler Freu - de! Es schwin-delt

fail,_____ A burn - ing fire de - vours me. None but the
mir,_____ es brennt mein Ein - ge - wei - de. Nur wer die

lone - ly heart Can know my sad - ness.
Sehn - sucht kennt, weiss, was ich lei - de!

I love thee
Ich liebe dich

Edvard Grieg

Ich lie - be dich wie nichts auf die-ser Er - den, ich lie - be dich, ich
I love thee more than an - y earth-ly crea-ture, I love thee, dear, I

lie - be dich, ich lie - be dich in Zeit und E - wig-keit! Ich
love thee, dear, I love thee now and for e - ter - ni - ty! I

lie - be dich in Zeit und E - wig-keit!
love thee now and for e - ter - ni - ty!

Ich den - ke dein, kann stets nur dei - ner den - ken, nur dei-nem
One thought of thee all oth - er thought drives from me, Pledged to thy

29

Were my song with wings provided
Si mes vers avaient des ailes

Reynaldo Hahn
Victor Hugo

wings   for   fly - ing,   Like   birds   of
vaient   des   ai - les,   Com -   me   l'oi-

air!   ing,   Un - to   thy   door   t'would   be
seau!   Ils   vo - le - raient,   é - tin-

hie   ing,   All   with   ten - der   greet - ings
cel   les,   Vers   vo - tre   foy - er   qui

fraught,_____   If   my   song   could   come   a   fly - ing
rit _____   Si   mes   vers   a -   vaient   des   ai - les

On wings of thought!
Com - me l'es - prit.

In thy heart to en-ter try - - ing, There it would stay ev-er
Près de vous, purs et fi - dè - les, Ils ac-cour-raient, nuit et

nigh,_____ Had my song but wings for fly-ing,
jour_____ Si mes vers a - vaient des ai - les,

Had my song but wings for fly - ing! Love too can fly!_____
Si mes vers a-vaient des ai - les Com - me l'a - mour!_____

Apres un Rêve

From the Tuscan, by Romain Bussine

Gabriel Fauré

Dans un som - meil__ que char - mait ton i -

ma - ge, Je rê - vais le bon - heur... ar - dent mi - ra - - -

ge; Tes yeux é - taient plus doux,__ ta voix pure et so - no - - re,

Tu ray - - on - nais comme un ciel___ é - clai - ré par l'au-

ro - - - re; Tu m'ap - pe -

lais___ et je quit - tais la ter - - re Pour m'en - fuir a - vec

toi vers la lu - miè - - - - re;

Les cieux pour nous en-tr'ou-vraient leurs nu - es, Splen -

cresc. poco a poco

deurs in - con - nu - es, Lu - eurs di - vi - nes en - tre -

cresc. poco a poco

vu - es. Hé - las! Hé - las, tris-te ré - veil des

dim.

son - - - ges, Je t'ap - pel - le,ô

mf

nuit,_____ rends-moi tes men - son - - - - - ges, Re-

viens, re - - viens ra - di - eu - - - -

se, Re - viens, ô nuit mys - té - ri -

eu - - - - - - - - se!

Last rose of summer

Qui sola, vergin rosa

Thomas Moore
Air: The Groves of Blarney

Andante con espresso

1.'Tis the last rose__ of__ sum - mer, Left__ bloom - ing a -
2.I'll not leave thee,__ thou__ lone one, To__ pine_____ on the
1. Qui__ so la,__ ver - gin ro - sa, come__ puoi__ tu fio -

lone;__ All her love - ly__ com - pan-ions Are__ fad - ed and
stem;__ Since the love - ly__ are__ sleep-ing, Go,__ sleep__ thou with
rir?__ An - co - ra mez-za-sco-sa, e__ pres - so gia a - mo

gone; No_ flow'r_ of her kin-dred, No rose_ -bud is
them. Thus kind - ly I'll scat - ter Thy leaves_ o'er the
rir!_ Non ha per - te ru - gia - de, già_ col - ta sei dal

nigh_ To re-flect back her_ blush-es, Or give_ sigh for
bed,_ Where thy mates of_ the_ gar-den Lie scent - less and
'gel!_ Il_ ca - po_ tuo già ca - de, Chi no_ sul ver - de

sigh.
dead.
stel!

3. So_ soon may I fol - low When friend - ships de -
2. Per *che so - la i - gno - ra - ta Lan - guir_ nel tuo giar -*

Drink to me only with thine eyes

Air by Colonel Mellish
1777 - 1817

ask a drink divine; But might I of Jove's nectar sup, I would not change for thine. I sent thee late a rosy wreath, Not so much honouring thee,

Now sleeps the crimson petal

Words by
Tennyson
Music by
Roger Quilter
Op. 3, No. 2

Now sleeps the crim-son pet - al, now the white;............

Nor waves the cy - press in the pal - ace walk;............

Nor winks the gold fin in the porph-'ry font: The

fire - fly wa - kens: wa - ken thou with

me.

with passion

Now folds the li - ly all her sweet-ness up,

And slips in - to the bo - som of the lake:............

So fold thy - self, my dear - est, thou, and slip,

pp ad lib.

slip In - to my bo - som and be lost,............ be

pp

cresc.

lost in me.

dying away

My mother bids me bind my hair

Bind' auf dein haar.

Canzonet.

Joseph Haydn

moth-er_ bids me bind_ my hair With bands_ of_ ros - y hue, Tie
auf Dein Haar, die Mut-ter spricht, und Bän - der win - de drein; mit

up___ my sleeves with rib - ands rare, And lace my bod - ice blue,
ro - sen - ro - then Schleifen licht, so schmück'Dein Mie - der fein,

Tie up___ my sleeves with rib - ands rare, And lace,___ and
mit ro - sen - ro - then Schlei - fen licht, so schmück', so

lace my_bod - ice blue. For
schmück' Dein Mie - der_ fein. Willst

why, she cries, sit still and weep, While oth - ers dance and
trau - ern Du, mein Kind, al - lein, weil Al - les tanzt so

play?
gern?
A - las! I scarce can
Ach, a - ber ach das

go or creep, While Lu - bin is a - way. A-
Her - ze mein seufzt: weh! mein Lieb' ist fern! Ach,

las! I scarce can go or creep, while Lu - bin is a - way, while
a - ber ach, das Her - ze mein seufzt: weh! mein Lieb' ist fern! mein

Lu - bin is a-way, is a - way, is a-way.
Lieb, mein Lieb' ist fern! Ist so fern! Ist so fern!

'Tis sad_ to think the days are gone, When those_ we love are near! I
O schö-ne Zeit, da Er_mir nah', den ein - zig ich_ ge-liebt, ich

sit_ up-on this mos - sy stone, And sigh when none can hear,
si - tze auf dem Stei - ne da und seuf-ze schwer be - trübt.

I sit_ up-on this mos - sy stone, and sigh,_ And sigh when none can
Ich si - tze auf dem Stei - ne da und seuf - ze, seuf - ze schwer be-